Edward William Cox

**Spiritualism Answered by Science**

Edward William Cox

**Spiritualism Answered by Science**

ISBN/EAN: 9783337334697

Printed in Europe, USA, Canada, Australia, Japan

Cover: Foto ©Lupo / pixelio.de

More available books at **www.hansebooks.com**

# SPIRITUALISM

# ANSWERED BY

# SCIENCE.

BY

EDWARD W. COX, S.L., F.R.G.S.

NEW YORK:

HENRY L. HINTON, PUBLISHER, 744 BROADWAY.

1872.

# PREFACE.

SOME of the Critics of the scientific experiments in Psychic Force, conducted with the aid of certain mechanical tests by Mr. CROOKES, F.R.S., in the presence of DR. HUGGINS, F.R.S., and myself, have erroneously assumed that we were converted by the results of those experiments to the creed of Spiritualism. The fact was the very reverse. Those experiments proved conclusively that the Force, supposed by many to be spiritual, is in fact a Force proceeding from the human organism.

But the anonymous writer of the article in the *Quarterly Review*, entitled "Spiritualism and its Recent Converts," cannot plead merely a mistake. He is guilty of deliberate falsehood in making that assertion, for he cites a passage from my letter to MR. CROOKES (so that he must have read it), in which letter I expressly thus state :—

> Allow me to add that I can find no evidence even tending to prove that the force is other than a force proceeding from or directly dependent upon the human organization, and therefore, as all other forces of nature, wholly within the province of that strictly scientific investigation to which you have been the first to subject it.

The crucial tests applied by the skill and science of Mr. Crookes confirmed the results of a series of other experiments, conducted with care and caution, which had been instituted for the purpose of investigating if any and what of the alleged phenomena were real : and, if real, whether they are physical or spiritual, natural or supernatural.

The conclusion from that patient inquiry has been, that many of the alleged phenomena are real, though some are delusions and others impostures ; that the Power dignified by the title of Spiritual, because attributed to the presence and action of spirits of the dead, is in fact a Psychic Force proceeding from the human structure and directed by the human intelligence.

But from what part of the human structure that Force proceeds—whether from nerve, ganglion, or brain—if it be the "vital force," or the "nerve ether" of Dr. Richardson—if the directing intel-

3

ligence is the "Unconscious Cerebration" of Dr. Carpenter, or if there be a Soul (or spirit) inhabiting the body and distinct from it, by which those effects are produced—are problems remaining for close, patient, and extensive research, by steadily pursuing the course of scientific investigation which MR. CROOKES has so successfully begun.

I am pleased to be enabled to state that, to promote this inquiry by discussion, disquisition and experiment, a Society is in progress of formation, to be called *The Psychological Society of Great Britain*, which should be joined by all who are interested in a subject the importance of which at this time it is impossible to exaggerate.

For Theology and modern Science are directly at issue as to the existence of a Soul in Man. Theology affirms and Science either denies or doubts, demanding proofs. If Psychic Force be the reality that they who have scientifically examined and tested it assert, it shakes to its foundation the materialism of modern Science, by the probability it raises that, *as a fact in Nature*, there is in us an entity, distinct from the corporeal structure, which can exercise an active force, directed by intel 'gence, beyond the limit of the bodily powers, and which is not material, but something other than that the scalpel carves and the microscope reveals.

The purposes of this brief treatise is to state fully and frankly the facts and arguments that have conducted to the conclusion that there *is* such a Force, and a non-corporeal something in us that controls it, and that Science may yet be enabled to restore the faith Science has shaken in the existence of the Soul and the consequent prospect of immortality.

*November* 25, 1871.

# CONTENTS.

# INTRODUCTORY.

SCIENCE is the natural enemy of Superstition.

A superstition is always founded on a fact. It is never wholly fanciful. Men note some facts in Nature they cannot at once explain and call them mysteries. These are the materials with which the imagination constructs a fabric of which one part is real and nine parts are visionary.

But a superstition founded on facts can only be overthrown by sapping its foundation, recognising the realities on which it rests, dragging them into the domain of Nature and Science, tearing away the veil of mystery, and showing that the facts, about which so much of the marvellous has been attracted, are in strict accordance with natural laws.

Science can successfuly combat Superstition only by strict observance of the great principle whose enunciation by Bacon made Science what it is—first, find *the fact*, then the conditions of its existence, and from this basis proceed to inquire into causes.

The argument *à priori* is equally foolish and fallacious. Modern Science was supposed to abjure it utterly. Her boast has been, that assertion that a thing *cannot* be because it is apparently opposed to some established law of nature, can never be accepted as an answer to averments of facts by credible persons which, according to the rules of evidence, would be accepted by any

judge or jury.   But Science is not bound to *believe* on
the testimony of witnesses, however competent and
credible.   The duty that devolves upon her in such
cases is to test by patient and careful examination the
truth of the fact so asserted; if, upon such fair and impartial trial it be found to be a fact, to proclaim it and
to show, as always may be shown, how that new fact
accords with the other facts of nature.

If such is the profession of modern Science, such is
not the practice.   On the contrary, hers is one long
history of practice in direct defiance of principle.   She
has met almost every new discovery by the old and, as
it was supposed, exploded argument *à priori*, instead of
by the Baconian rule of first ascertaining the fact and
then arguing upwards from it.   As the necessary con-
sequence she has been put to shame continually.   The
circulation of the blood, vaccination, express trains,
Atlantic steaming, and a host of other novelties, were
as vehemently opposed by the scientific authorities in
their time as now is Mr. Crookes's announcement of
certain physiological facts observed by him, and by the
self-same argument *à priori*—that they are inconsistent
with recognised natural laws and therefore *cannot* be.

Mr. Crookes does not ask their acceptance on his own
authority; he asks only that the experiments he has
tried—and which, if established, are of the highest interest and importance to Science—may be tried by
others.   He describes them in plain words made more
plain by engravings.   He says :—

The answer to this, as to all other objections, is, prove it to be an
error by showing where the error lies ; or, if a trick, by showing
how the trick is performed.   Try the experiment fully and fairly.

**If then fraud be found, expose it ; if it be a truth, proclaim it. This is the only scientific procedure, and this it is that I purpose steadily to pursue.'**

Not one of the many objectors to his demonstration of the existence of a Psychic Force has ventured to answer him by saying, "I have tried the experiments described by Mr. Crookes, carefully and patiently, and the results he stated did not appear." All have shrunk from this only philosophical treatment of the question. The warfare has been wholly by suppression of one half of the facts stated by him and misrepresentation of the other half; and some have even condescended to personal abuse and vilification, for the purpose of discrediting testimony they are unable to rebut. A few instances must suffice.

The *Quarterly Review* answers a series of experiments made with instruments ingeniously constructed by a scientific man to secure delicate tests that should not be open to the objection that would have been made to any evidence of the senses alone, by the unworthy process of discrediting the experimentalist and observers. Mr. Crookes, F.R.S., the discoverer of the metal thallium, the Editor of the *Quarterly Journal of Science* and of the *Chemical News*, is declared to be incompetent to devise a simple test apparatus ; Dr. Huggins, F.R.S., a Vice-President of the Royal Society, the foremost spectroscopist in the world and almost its greatest astronomer, is wanting in power of vision and capacity of judgment ; (a) and my much humbler self, a

---

(a) Dr. Huggins is actually condemned by the *Quarterly Review* for having dared be a witness to some mechanical experiments without having first studied Dr. Carpenter's theory of "Unconscious Cere-

Lawyer of some little experience in dealing with witnesses and evidence, am called " gullible " (a). We

bration." " To him;" says the Reviewer, " seeing is believing ; but to those who have qualified themselves for the study of Psychic Force by a previous course of investigation into the class of occult phenomena, of which this is the latest manifestation, seeing is anything but believing."

(a) The silly story referred to as the sole foundation for this insulting attack is simply that many years ago, when I was a Law Student, mesmerism, which is now, under the name of somnambulism, accepted by all physiologists as a fact, was as fiercely supported and opposed as is Psychism at present. There was a boy called Goble, who was a somnambulist, and in his sleep-walking exhibited some of the most remarkable phenomena of that condition—such as doing delicate work, writing, and seeming to read, in the dark with his eyes closed. A friend who shared my chambers had taken great interest in the subject, and thither the boy was brought for experiment if somnambulism could be artificially produced. He was speedily thrown into the sleep, and in this state of *artificial* somnambulism, he not only did all that had been observed in his natural sleep-walking state, but much besides equally curious. He was subjected to experimental examination for some weeks by Dr. Elliotson, Dr. Marsden, and many other physiologists, who were satisfied of the genuineness of his condition. Frequently he read words enclosed in five or six envelopes of thick brown paper, each one being sealed; and, with a handful of cotton wool over each eye, and two handkerchiefs bound over that, he read the advertisements in the *Times* with perfect ease and fluency. In fact, he did in the somnambulist condition artificially produced what he had done in his natural sleep-walking condition. Dr. Forbes, hearing of the case from his scientific friends, expressed a great wish to see the boy, and asked us as a favour to procure for him an interview. Confiding in fair dealing, this was done, and Dr. Forbes came, bringing with him Mr. Sharpey. No intimation was given that they had designed *a trap*. Dr. Forbes had asked only to try *a test*. They brought with them a box. The boy was told by them that it contained some writing, and that if he would read it they would give him a sovereign. The box was placed in his hand. Not improbably there were some arrangements are, in fact, three fools, and all this dirt is thrown for the paltry purpose of discrediting our attestation to the *good faith* with which certain experiments were tried by Mr. Crookes, and to which Dr. Huggins, as a man peculiarly versed in the construction and use of

---

within the box which affected the conditions necessary to perception ; or it may be no writing there at all.  However that may have been, the boy, after long trial, said that it was useless—he could not "see" (that was his term for the perceptive power he had) what was in the box.  Upon this his two visitors plied him the more with promises ; if he would but try again and read the writing, they would give him *two* pounds—they would publish his name in all the papers, and make his fortune.  Having thus stimulated him to the utmost, they proposed that we should retire and leave him alone, telling him that he should have a quarter of an hour by himself to make it out. He was left alone.  The box appeared easy to open—only a sliding cover.  Tempted by the great reward offered to him, and the power failing, he tried to open the box.  This was what the visitors had desired and designed.  They had made a trap and baited it.  The cover so temptingly left unfastened was held by a thread which, by its severance, marked any attempted opening of it.  It was plain that he had made the attempt.  To those who had seen him times out of number read words in sealed envelopes that had *not* been broken, and *could not* have been broken without detection, one endeavour to draw back an apparently unfastened cover under the stimulus of lavish promises was, of course, no proof whatever that everything he had before done, under the conditions that made peeping *impossible*, was imposture ; and Dr. Forbes was called upon, as a matter of justice to the boy and to science, to make further trial in a manner more fair and under the same conditions of sealed envelopes of paper which had satisfied the many other scientific men who had tested him.  But, fearing to have his verdict reversed on a new trial, he refused it.

And this is the incident, that happened nearly *thirty* years ago, for which I am declared, in the most insulting language, to be *now* an incompetent witness to the motion of an index to which a board was suspended.

scientific apparatus, and myself as a person experienced in the art of testing truth and detecting falsehood, were invited to be witnesses, merely to observe and to detect whatever results might be exhibited by certain machinery. Surely this was not an offence calling for *personal* vilification. The Old Bailey practice " If you cannot answer the facts, abuse the prosecutor and his witnesses," ought not to be admitted into scientific controversy. When Mr. Crookes announced his discovery of a new metal, when Dr. Huggins published his observations of the new lines in the spectrum, they were not met by the assertion that they were incompetent or untrustworthy, their apparatus worthless, their eyes deceivers, and their senses and judgments befooled; but the men of science hastened to try the same experiments, and ascertain, by their own investigation, what truth there was in what Dr. Huggins and Mr. Crookes had asserted. Why, therefore, are these gentlemen to be maligned and vilified now for asserting that other experiments had exhibited other new facts, and for asking that Science should deal with the alleged discovery of Psychic Force precisely as it had dealt with the discoveries of the spectroscope.

It has been stated in some of the newspapers that Dr. Carpenter is the author of the article in the *Quarterly Review*. I am reluctant to believe it. He is reputed to be a gentleman, and certainly no person pretending to that title could, even in the conflict of rival theories, have forgotten that the intellectual reputation of scientific men is very dear to them, and should not have been thus vilified by another scientific man for so paltry an object as the discrediting of one of their experiments.

Dr. Carpenter, moreover, is, least of any man, entitled so to treat other propounders of new theories. If Dr. Carpenter rejects and ridicules Mr. Crookes's demonstrations of Psychic Force, at least an equal amount of ridicule is cast by other physiologists on Dr. Carpenter's conjectural theory of " *Unconscious Cerebration.*" The evidence that supports the assertion of a Psychic Force by Mr. Crookes is vastly more trustworthy and demonstrative than that adduced by Dr. Carpenter in support of what so many of his brother Scientists call his "*gobe-moucherie.*" He forgets that in *their* estimation he is himself, if not the *most* gullible (for that, he says, am I), the most gullible save one, for accepting as facts the wonderful stories on which he founds his much boasted theory of "Unconscious Cerebration." (*a*) For the honour of science, I hope yet to be assured that Dr. Carpenter was not the writer of the article in question, or that no unworthy jealousy of the reputation of brother Scientists prompted a personal attack upon them, so ungenerous, so unjust, and so uncalled for.

The *Saturday Review* was even more unfair alike to the experiments and the experimentalists. It indulged, on this occasion, beyond its wont, in the *suppressio veri* as well as in the *suggestio falsi*. It did not describe the experiments truly. It sought to discredit them by the familiar process of misrepresenting them. This could not have been mere misunderstanding, for the descrip-

---

(*a*) For my own part, I do not share the ridicule showered by physiologists on Dr. Carpenter and his discovery. I entirely accept his theory, and I think I see in it a solution of the problem how the Psychic Force demonstrated by Mr. Crookes is controlled and directed.

tions were in plain words, made more plain by engravings.

Here also the contrivance was resorted to of endeavouring to discredit the experiment by disparaging the experimentalist and his witnesses. Here, too, the unscientific practice was adopted of answering a fact asserted by honourable and intelligent men by the argument—" it is apparently opposed to something which I (the writer) accept as truth, therefore it cannot be; and you, the asserters of it, are liars or fools, wilfully deluding others or weakly self-deluded."

The *Athenæum* was not far behind its fellows in this species of warfare. It was not, like them, abusive—it was even civil in tone and language. But it went beyond them in misrepresentation, misquotation, and fallacious reasoning. It would take many pages to expose all the errors of that article, but one will suffice as a specimen of the whole:

The story of the dining-room table is told in two different ways ; the drawers of the report give one, Mr. Serjeant Cox gives another version of the affair. . . . . The dimensions of the tables operated on by the committee are thus given in the report : "The smallest of them was 5ft. 9in. long by 4ft. wide, the largest 9ft. 3in. long by 4½ft. wide, and of proportionate weight. . . . . Mr. Serjeant Cox, on the contrary, states the dimensions of the top of the table to be 12ft. by 5ft.

Now what is the *fact?* If the reviewer had *read* what he was reviewing, he would have seen that the contradiction existed only in his own brain. The experiment referred to by Mr. Sergeant Cox is dated in his memorandum, appended to the report of sub-committee No. 1, and was made at a different date and place from the experiments reported by the committee. The latter closed in May, 1869, the former took place in January, 1871, and the table was not the same as those referred to by the committee. Moreover, all the reviewers conveniently omit the fact, stated in the report, that Dr. Edmonds, whose authority they use so eagerly as a dissentient from the report of the investigation sub-committee, was not present at any one of their meetings, and did not witness any one of the forty experiments which convinced all who did witness them; his objections being, like those of the reviewers, merely an argument why the alleged facts *could* not be, instead of the only answer Science can approve, "I attended with you, and watched the experiments you describe, and, after a full, fair, and patient trial, I failed to find the results you assert."

Another part of the article in the *Athenæum* cannot be passed without notice. Eleven persons of intelligence, social position, in full possession of their senses, in the light of gas, and in the dining-room of Dr. Edmonds, saw his dining-table, which is unusually long and heavy, moved many times in succession over a space of several feet, without contact, or possibility of contact, by any person present, and in one of these lurches, by the force of its motion, it knocked down a lady who chanced to be standing in its way. Yet the *Athenæum* resorts to the wretched explanation of this well-attested phenomenon that all the eleven persons present were deceived by their senses, and that the table did not really move at all! Could scientific dogmatism further go? I should like to see the writer of this piece of nonsense addressing his argument to a jury in a court of justice. "Gentlemen, eleven witnesses have told us that they were standing together in a well-lighted room, at a distance of three feet from a dining-table, twelve feet long and five feet wide, and that this table swung round untouched by any of them, and knocked down a lady who was in its way. I cannot impute to these witnesses intentional falsehood, but I contend that they were mistaken—that the table never moved at all, and I ask you to find a verdict accordingly." What a shout of derisive laughter would greet such an argument in the court, and what ridicule would be cast upon it in the journals. Yet that which would be scouted from any court of justice in the world is gravely advanced by men who call themselves "scientific," and think themselves sensible, and is accepted and printed, without consciousness of its utter absurdity, by the editor of a literary journal!

It is due to another class, of which the *Spectator* is an eminent example, to acknowledge the fairness and the gentlemanly tone of commentaries, which were, in substance—"We cannot accept the fact as determined by your experiments, but you have stated enough to require from competent persons a careful and patient scientific examination, with further tests and under other conditions."

And this is all that Mr. Crookes asks for himself, and that the report of the Dialectical Society recommends.

I pass now to the question to which this little treatise is devoted.

*Is* there a Force which, in the presence of certain persons, without corporeal contact or connection, can cause motion in heavy bodies, and produce audible sounds, as by impact, which appears sometimes to be directed by intelligence?

If there be such a Force in fact, whence does it proceed?

Is it, as Spiritualism asserts, the operation of spirits of the dead?

Or is it, as contended by Mr. Crookes and other scientific experimentalists, a force emanating from, or in some manner directly dependent on, the human organisation?

The following pages propose, first, to state the proved phenomena, and then to set forth the reasons that have led to the conclusion that the force is a purely Psychic Force, and *not* the work of spirits of the dead.

It is objected to this inquiry that, if proved, the knowledge would be worthless. I answer by asking— Is any knowledge of a new fact in nature without its use? Does any fact stand alone? Does not the discovery of one fact invariably lead to the discovery of an endless series of other facts that grow out of it? Are we so far advanced in our knowledge of Psychology, or even of Physiology, that it can be no help to these sciences to learn that the Force which performs all the functions of organisation operates in certain cases beyond the boundary of the living body? If this fact be established, it needs no stretch of imagination to anticipate its multifold application to the solution of many of the now insoluble problems connected with the relationship of mind and body, the laws of life and health, and the science and practice of medicine.

It has been gravely asked by some of our critics, what right have I, a practical Lawyer, to concern myself about science? My authority as a witness to a simple mechanical experiment has been impugned on a plea of the incapacity of a Lawyer to understand the principles or observe the phenomena of science. I answer this objection by reference to Mr. Grove, Q. C., at once a great lawyer and a great Scientist; to Mr. Gwyn Jeffrey, who has devoted his leisure to natural history; to Lord Brougham, who wrote on optics, and others whom it is not necessary to enumerate. It might be permitted to a very much humbler man than they to give some of his hours of leisure, as I have preferred to do, to the study of the sciences that relate to the mind—to Mental Philosophy and Psychology. However that may be, the practical knowledge of the principles of evidence, the daily habit of looking for the very truth, without prejudice, fear or favour, combined with long practical experience in the art of sifting and weighing proofs before forming an opinion, might by some be deemed rather a qualification than otherwise for careful observation, and arriving at a fair judgment of what fact is true, what false, what real and what imagination or imposture.

I can only say, as an expert, that if the evidence of the existence of Psychic Force, produced under so many and various conditions, with such careful experiments and under tests so often repeated, is not to be deemed a sufficient proof of the fact that motions of heavy bodies and audible sounds of impact upon them are produced without contact or material connection with any person present (for that is all we assert), however that fact may be explained, the pursuit of truth must be abandoned as hopeless. If the senses of honest and intelligent observers are not to be trusted for a fact so obvious to the eye as that of a table being moved untouched over spaces of several feet, how is the common business of life to be conducted? We must close our courts of justice, for upon evidence infinitely more disputable than that attested by the scientific experimentalists and the Investigation Committee, liberty and property are daily dealt with by all our tribunals. If the argument of the critics be right, we must henceforth banish the witnesses who depose to what they have seen and heard, and try men for life and liberty on á priori argument alone, ignoring the evidence of facts and reasoning on what can or cannot be, according to the conjectures, the assumptions and the theories of Scientists.

Much prejudice has been raised against the experiments that have demonstrated the existence of Psychic Force by a prevalent belief that the phenomena occur only in the presence of a few professional Psychics, and the suspicion of imposture thus suggested. This popular error will probably account for much of the unreasoning abuse that has been cast upon its assertors, such as was not displayed towards the investigators of any other of the forces of nature, however strange and novel were the phenomena described and in their first aspect inexplicable. But, in fact, Psychics are frequent in private life. There are few family circles in which some of the phenomena of Psychism might not be exhibited on patient trial. All the forty experimental meetings of the sub-committee of the Dialectical Society, and almost all the further ex-

periments here reported, were conducted with Psychics
found in private life, among personal friends and
acquaintances, and *not* with professional, paid, or public
Psychics, as it has been wrongly assumed. Psychic
Force is often developed to an extraordinary extent in
children too young to be capable of contriving or conducting an elaborate fraud, and too weak to possess the
requisite muscular power to move a heavy table. With
*all* Psychics the phenomena simply occur in their
presence, without effort of their own will to promote
or check them, and, as all agree, without the slightest
consciousness of any attendant sensation, bodily or
mental.

And by whom are the facts thus powerfully attested
denied? *By those only who have never tried and proved
them.* If they are *not* facts, but delusions and impostures, how comes it that not a single investigator of
repute, after patient and honest examination, has failed
to be convinced that the phenomena are real, or
ventured to assert that he has discovered a trick and
shown how it was effected? It is probable, nay,
possible, that if they were really the feats of conjurors,
the manner of performing them would not have been
discovered by some one of the many witnesses eager
to dissipate a delusion? Half-a-dozen visits suffice to
enable even a stupid spectator to detect the *modus
operandi* of the cleverest conjurors ever seen among us;
and every trick is to be found fully described in books,
and may be successfully performed by any person
willing to take a little trouble in the learning. But
Psychics of all classes, of both sexes, and of all ages,
have been observed for thirty years by thousands of /

persons, sitting at the same table with them and
holding their hands and feet, and *in no single instance*
has ingenuity or accident discovered the contrivance
(if it be one) by which what is seen and heard is performed. Has it never occurred to the critics that if
Psychics can do by slight of hand or mechanical
agency what any person may daily witness if he pleases,
they have no need to remain for a day unknown and
poor. The skill that could accomplish what takes
place in their presence, under the vigilant eyes with
which they are encompassed, would speedily secure for
them an enormous fortune as mechanicians, or an
unbounded popularity and profit as prestidigitateurs.

Not only is the evidence by which the phenomena of
Psychic Force are established stronger than any upon
which the criminal courts daily convict and punish
even with death; it is at least equal to the evidence
upon which most of the other sciences are founded.
The experiments with Psychic Force are in all respects
as perfect and trustworthy as those exhibited by
Professor Tyndall at the Royal Institution. They are
as plain to the eye, as palpable to the touch, as audible
to the ear, as any witnessed in that famous lecture room.
If the senses can deceive in the one, so are they equally
liable to be deceived in the other, and the argument of
imposture would be found equally applicable to both.
The experiment of the Psychic Force requires certain
conditions for its production ; so do Dr. Tyndall's experiments. Those conditions failing, the experiment
fails, alike with the Psychic and with the Professor. It
is a favourite argument with opponents of Psychic
Force, "If it can be done thus, why not *thus ?*" Put

the same question to Professor Tyndall ; he would confess that *his* experiments also are subject to conditions,
and that *he* could not engage to perform one of them if
conditions other than his own were imposed upon him.
Occasional failure is a frequent objection to Psychic
Force. But the Professor also fails often. Many a
time I have heard him say to his audience, after a
failure which opponents might call suspicious, " I tried
this experiment in my laboratory just before the
lecture and it succeeded admirably. It fails now, I
know not why. There are some unfavourable conditions I cannot discover. These disappointments are
frequent in science. Nature dictates her own conditions ; we cannot impose them upon her." But when
the like failure occurs with an experiment in Psychism,
and the same reason is assigned for it, opponents ex-
claim at once—" Manifest imposture ! It failed when
we sceptics determined the conditions. If it could
be done at one time, it could be done at another time."
Yet in what single particular does the case of the
Psychic differ from that of the Professor ? What
better assurance have we that the experiments we
behold with so much amazement from the benches of
the Royal Institution are genuine ? Nothing would
be so easy as imposture *there.* With his attendant for
a confederate, a little sleight of hand, and some ingenious mechanism, all that Professor Tyndall declares
that he does might be imposed upon us, and a clever
trick passed off as a new fact in nature. You ask what
could be the motive for such a deceit ? The answer is
that the Professor is *paid* for lecturing ; that is the objection made to experiments with Psychics as honest

and honourable as Professor Tyndall. But most of the Psychics are in fact *unpaid*, and therefore they are really *less* open to the suspicion of unworthy motive than is the Professor.

It is not expected, it is not asked, of any person to accept the existence of Psychic Force on faith of the sufficiency of the experiments by which conviction of its reality was carried to those who witnessed them. They ask only that other competent observers should pursue a similar course of patient examination, and report if they also find the phenomena to be facts, and if the facts they find point to the like conclusion, or what other explanation of them suggests itself to their minds. The first step in science is to ascertain, without fear or favour, what are *the facts*, satisfied that, however strange or conflicting with established theories these facts may appear at first, they will assuredly be found, on further investigation, to be in strict accordance with every other fact, and to square with every truthful theory.

Who would have supposed that in these days of free inquiry such extreme irritability could be exhibited by the Professors of Physical Science at the bare suggestion of the possible existence of something in man that cannot be carved by the scalpel, seen by the microscope, and analysed in the laboratory? Who could have anticipated the virulence of hostility with which they pursue all who venture to assert that there may be psychological facts, dependent on psychological conditions and governed by psychological laws, distinct from, and but imperfectly controlled by, those material laws to which alone their useful labours are devoted. Unhappily there is a fanaticism of scepticism as well as a

fanaticism of faith. Dogmatism is at least as rampant
in science as in theology. A true Materialist would
be sorely vexed if it could be demonstrated to him
that he has an immortal soul. I cannot help suspecting that this endeavour to deter even from inquiry by
anticipatory denunciation as fools or rogues of all who
dare to inquire, is prompted by a suspicion lurking in
a corner of the minds of the Materialist Philosophers
that there may be some truth after all in this evidence
of a Psychic Force: and that, if a truth, it will go far
to disturb their favourite dogma, that mind is a secre-
tion of the body; that life is an arrangement of particles;
that there is nothing of us but doth perish and pass
away; that we are only animated machines that perform a prescribed task, fall to pieces, and there end.
I cannot disguise from them, from the reader, or from
myself, that if the existence of a Psychic Force is the
*fact* which, after most careful and anxious examination, I am satisfied that *it is*, and of which I ask others
to satisfy themselves by a like investigation, it *does* go
very far indeed to disturb the Philosophy of Materialism which has taken so strong a hold of the scientific
world, by the probability it raises that there is a something in man, other than the visible material body,
from which that Force proceeds, or with which it is intimately associated.

But, however adverse may be the Materialists to
investigations into facts in nature, tending to prove that
they and we have an *anima*, *soul* (whatever name be
given to it), and the probability of a future existence
which such a possession would undoubtedly go far to
confirm, not merely as a dogma in theology, but as *a*

*fact in nature,* the question will be admitted to be of overwhelming interest. Apart from the new light which the existence of Psychic Force, if proved, must throw upon many of the obscurities of physiology and medicine, the establishment of its truth will open a new field to psychological science, give to religion a new strength, and encourage in millions hopes and aspirations which, reluctant though they may be to confess it even to themselves, have been painfully shaken by the materialism of modern science.

To conclude this long, but I hope not irrelevant, introduction, I add a summary of the argument :

A protracted series of careful experiments has proved the existence of certain phenomena.

These phenomena appear to indicate the existence of a *Force,* hitherto unrecognised, proceeding from the human organisation.

The asserted phonomena are true or false.

If true, they demand investigation in order to ascertain their origin; if they sustain the suggestion of a Psychic Force, or, if not, to what other source can they be traced ?

If false, they should be exploded for ever, not by mere denial, but by detection and exposure of the contrivances by which they are produced.

In the one case, the world will profit by an enormous addition to human knowledge.

In the other case, it will be benefited by the banishment of a vast amount of superstition and imposture.

For either end, the duties of Science are the same— a careful, extensive, patient and unprejudiced examination.

## THE PHENOMENA.

WHEN the London Dialectical Society resolved to appoint a committee to examine and report upon the pretensions of Spiritualism, I entered upon its duties, in common with five-sixths of the members of that committee, having the most firm conviction that we should detect a fraud or dissipate a delusion. I hoped that long experience in the work of sifting and weighing evidence, and resolving what does or does not constitute proof of asserted facts, would enable me to do good service in detecting imposture and discovering its contrivances. And such were the aims and the expectations of the great majority of my colleagues, comprising men of various pursuits and capacities, ingenious lawyers, practised scientists, skilful doctors, authors, artists, and shrewd men of business—all of them persons with keen senses, proved powers of observation, suspecting and looking for imposition, and therefore more than commonly vigilant with eye and ear and rigid in the application of tests.

Before we commenced to examine, it was our confident belief that the alleged phenomena were:

1. Self-delusion by the spectator; or,
2. Imposture by the Psychic; or,
3. Involuntary and unconscious muscular action.

With our minds thus prejudiced against the reality of the phenomena, we proceeded to their investigation.

### INVESTIGATION BY THE SUB-COMMITTEE OF THE DIALECTICAL SOCIETY.

It was resolved that we should meet only at the private residences of members of the committee, so as to preclude all possible pre-arrangement of mechanism or other contrivances.

That no professional medium should be employed.

That careful notes should be taken of each experiment and signed for verification by all present.

A Psychic was found in the person of a Lady, the wife of one of the members of the general committee, of high professional and social position. In this we were pre-eminently fortunate, for the Lady in question had never witnessed any of the phenomena with others, and therefore could not have mastered the sleight of hand, requiring the practice of a life for its mastery, which would be necessary for the successful performance of a trick, if trick it was. In truth, she had discovered their production in her own presence only by chance, a few weeks previously to acceding to the request of the sub-committee to assist them in their investigations.

But three or four only of the forty experimental meetings of the committee were held at this Lady's house; all the other meetings were held at the houses of members, and some of them at my own residence; so that I can affirm positively the absence of any mechanical or other pre-arranged contrivances by which the phenomena there witnessed could have been produced.

### IS IT DELUSION OR FRAUD?

We were speedily satisfied that it was not a delusion

of the senses. The sounds were distinctly audible to
the ear, the vibrations palpable to the touch, and the
motions obvious to sight. It was not a question of
doubtful mental impression only, but of actual measurement. The table and other pieces of furniture had
changed their position by so many inches, feet, yards.
There could be no possible mistake as to this fact of
motion. We were compelled to dismiss our theory
that it was a *self-delusion.*

But the motion and sounds may have been produced
by trickery and fraud. That was our second theory.
Accordingly we assumed the office of detectives. We
sat under the table while the motions and sounds were
most vigorous. We held the hands and feet of the
Psychic. Every hand in the circle was held by its
neighbour; the gas was bright above us; not a finger
could have stirred without being perceived by some of
the many eyes that were keeping watch. Our ingenuity was exercised in the invention and application of
tests. *After trials often repeated we were compelled to
confess that imposture was out of the question.* The motions and sounds were undoubtedly real, and were certainly not caused by any trickery.

### Is it Unconscious Muscular Action?

We retreated then upon the third theory, boasting
Faraday as its parent, and repeated ever since by objectors, who had not seen them, as the easy and sufficient
explanation of the phenomena we were witnessing—
namely, involuntary and unconscious action of the
muscles of those by whom the heavy body was touched.
" Here," we said, " are eighty fingers upon the table.

If each one exerts but a pressure so slight as to be imperceptible even to themselves, the aggregate sum of pressure will be very considerable. Apply these multiplied pressures at the edge of the table, and every finger is converted into a lever of which the centre of the table is the fulcrum. Make trial of it and it will be found so to be. That the muscles will act unconsciously there can be no doubt; and after a lengthened resting of the hand in a constrained position there is involuntary contraction of the muscles sufficient by the accumulated force to cause motion of the table, even though every person present should scrupulously endeavour to avoid pressure."

Such was the reasonable argument that led us to look to involuntary muscular action as the explanation of the motions and sounds that were continually being made. To ascertain if this hypothesis was correct, we devised a series of tests that should place the matter beyond all possible doubt. First, all hands were laid upon the table; then one hand only of each person; then the table was touched by the tips only of all the fingers; then by the fingers of one hand alone; then with one finger only. Still the motions and sounds continued with but slightly diminished force. If our theory of involuntary pressure was correct, the force should have diminished in precise proportion to the lessened points of contact. Moreover, it did not explain the fact, continually before our eyes, of the table being raised several inches from the floor on one side only, the muscular action of the fingers upon that side of the table being antagonistic and not contributory to such a motion! We continued our experiments with lessened faith in our foregone conclusion. First, one person withdrew from all contact; then a second, and a third, until one finger of one person only touched the table. Nevertheless it moved, the sounds continued to come from it, and a frequent motion was the lifting up of the table at the side on which the finger was pressing down, if exercising any pressure whatever. I should state that at all of these test experiments the tables employed were the large and heavy dining tables, some nine feet and some twelve feet long, with six legs, in common daily use in the dining-room of members of the committee, standing upon Turkey carpets, therefore not easily slid and difficult to move by the arm. We next tried a more decisive test. All hands were joined and held over the table at the height of three inches from it, no part of any hand touching it, the room being well lighted with gas and all eyes keeping careful watch over the lifted hands. The sounds were heard and the motions produced as before. It was suggested that possibly the feet might be at work; so two of the members seated themselves under the table to observe. The motions and sounds continued, but not a foot stirred. Then all the persons present stood, so that *no* foot could touch the table unseen. Still it moved. Lastly we devised a test that conclusively settled the question as to the possible agency of muscular action, conscious or unconscious. It was contrived thus: All present turned the backs of their chairs to the table, and kneeling upon the chairs, placed their arms upon the backs of the chairs, their hands being extended above the table, but without possibility of contact with it. The chairs were first placed six inches from the

table, with which, as the reader will readily understand, neither foot nor hand, nor any part of the person,
of any of those present could possibly come into contact unseen. In this position the table moved eight
inches over the carpet and tilted several times. The
chairs were then withdrawn further from the table, on
each trial to an increased distance, and with the same
results. At the distance of two feet from it the motions
were continued, with but slightly diminished power. I
must repeat that this was tried in the dining-rooms or
members, some of them in my own house, with none
present but the Committee and the Psychic. These
experiments of motion without contact were repeated
many times at different meetings in different houses,
and with the same results. Thus was our third and last
explanatory conjecture, which we had eagerly accepted
on the authority of Faraday, completely demolished
by the facts, and we were compelled reluctantly to
the conclusion that there is a Force apparently proceeding from the human organisation by which motion is
produced in heavy substances without the employment
of any muscular force, and without contact or material
connection of any kind between such substances and
the body of any person present. We agreed also that
these sounds and motions were directed, frequently by
some intelligence ; but as the duty of the committee
was merely to ascertain the facts, and not to inquire
into causes, with these conclusive proofs of the physical
facts we closed the investigation and reported accordingly.

As many of the reviewers have suppressed the most
interesting and important part of the volume, the report

of the sub-committee, No. 1, appointed to examine the phenomena experimentally and test it carefully, and which held no less than forty meetings for that purpose, of each of which meetings a report appears in the appendix, I introduce here the entire of that Report :—

Since their appointment on the 16th February, 1869, your sub-committee have held *forty* meetings for the purpose of experiment and test.

All of these meetings were held at the private residences of members of the committee, purposely to preclude the possibility of pre-arranged mechanism or contrivance.

The furniture of the room in which the experiments were conducted was on every occasion its accustomed furniture.

The tables were in all cases heavy dining tables, requiring a strong effort to move them. The smallest of them was 5ft. 9in. long by 4ft. wide, and the largest, 9ft. 3in. long and 4½ft. wide, and of proportionate weight.

The rooms, tables, and furniture generally were repeatedly subjected to careful examination before, during, and after the experiments, to ascertain that no concealed machinery, instrument, or other contrivance existed by means of which the sounds or movements hereinafter mentioned could be caused.

The experiments were conducted in the light of gas, except on the few occasions specially noted in the minutes.

Your committee have avoided the employment of professional or paid mediums, the mediumship being that of members of your sub-committee, persons of good social position and of unimpeachable integrity, having no pecuniary object to serve, and nothing to gain by deception.

Your committee have held some meetings without the presence of a medium (it being understood that throughout this report the word "medium" is used simply to designate an individual without whose presence the phenomena described either do not occur at all, or with greatly diminished force and frequency), purposely to try if they could produce, by any efforts effects similar to those witnessed when a medium was present. By no endeavours were they enabled to produce anything at all resembling the manifestations which took place in the presence of a medium.

Every test that the combined intelligence of your committee could devise has been tried with patience and perseverance. The experiments were conducted under a great variety of conditions, and ingenuity has been exerted in devising plans by which your committee might verify their observations and preclude the possibility of imposture or of delusion.

Your committee have confined their reports to *facts* witnessed by them in their collective capacity, which facts were *palpable to the senses, and their reality capable of demonstrative proof.*

Of the members of your sub-committee about *four-fifths* entered upon the investigation wholly sceptical as to the reality of the alleged phenomena, firmly believing them to be the result either of *imposture* or of *delusion*, or of *involuntary muscular action*. It was only by irresistible evidence under conditions that precluded the possibility of either of these solutions, and after trial and test many times repeated, that the most sceptical of your sub-committee were slowly and reluctantly convinced that the phenomena exhibited in the course of their protracted inquiry were veritable facts.

The result of their long-continued and carefully-conducted experiments, after trial by every detective test they could devise, has been to establish conclusively :

First : That under certain bodily or mental conditions of one or more of the persons present, a force is exhibited sufficient to set in motion heavy substances, without the employment of any muscular force, without contact or material connection of any kind between such substances and the body of any person present.

Second : That this force can cause sounds to proceed, distinctly audible to all present, from solid substances not in contact with, nor having any visible or material connection with, the body of any person present, and which sounds are proved to proceed from such substances by the vibrations which are distinctly felt when they are touched.

Third : That this force is frequently directed by intelligence.

At *thirty-four* out of the forty meetings of your committee some of these phenomena occurred.

A description of one experiment, and the manner of conducting it, will best show the care and caution with which your committee have pursued their investigations.

So long as there was contact, or even the possibility of contact, by the hands or feet, or even by the clothes of any person in the room, with the substance moved or sounded, there could be no perfect assurance that the motions and sounds were not produced by the person so in contact. The following experiment was therefore tried :

On an occasion when eleven members of your sub-committee had been sitting round one of the dining-tables above described for forty minutes, and various motions and sounds had occurred, they, by way of test, turned the backs of their chairs to the table, at about nine inches from it. They all then knelt upon their chairs, placing their arms upon the backs thereof. In this position, their feet were of course turned away from the table, and by no possibility could be placed under it or touch the floor. The hands of each person were extended over the table at about four inches from the surface. Contact, therefore, with any part of the table could not take place without detection.

In less than a minute the table, untouched, moved *four* times ; at first about *five* inches to one side, then about *twelve* inches to the opposite side, and then, in like manner, four inches and six inches respectively.

The hands of all present were next placed on the backs of their chairs, and about a foot from the table, which again moved, as before, *five* times, over spaces varying from four to six inches. Then all the chairs were removed twelve inches from the table, and each person knelt on his chair as before, this time however folding his hands behind his back, his body being thus about eighteen inches from the table, and having the back of the chair between himself and the table. The table again moved four times, in various directions. In the course of this conclusive experiment, and in less than half-an-hour, the table thus moved, without contact or possibility of of contact with any person present, thirteen times, the movements being in different directions, and some of them according to the request of various members of your sub-committee.

The table was then carefully examined, turned upside down and taken to pieces, but nothing was discovered to account for the phenomena. The experiment was conducted throughout in the full light of gas above the table.

Altogether, your sub-committee have witnessed upwards of *fifty* similar motions without contact on *eight* different evenings, in the houses of members of your sub-committee, the most careful tests being applied on each occasion.

In all similar experiments the possibility of mechanical or other contrivance was further negatived by the fact that the movements were in various directions—now to one side, then to the other ; now up the room, now down the room—motions that would have required the co-operation of many hands or feet ; and these, from the great size and weight of the tables, could not have been so used without the visible exercise of muscular force. Every hand and foot was plainly to be seen, and could not have been moved without instant detection.

Delusion was out of the question. The motions were in various directions, and were witnessed simultaneously by all present. They were matters of measurement, and not of opinion or of fancy.

And they occurred so often, under so many and such various conditions, with such safeguards against error or deception, and with such invariable results, as to satisfy the members of your sub-committee by whom the experiments were tried, wholly sceptical as most of them were when they entered upon the investigation, that *there is a force capable of moving heavy bodies without material contact, and which force is in some unknown manner dependent upon the presence of human beings.*

Your sub-committee have not, collectively, obtained any evidence as to the nature and source of this force, but simply as to *the fact of its existence.*

There appears to your committee to be no ground for the popular belief that the presence of sceptics interferes in any manner with the production or action of the force.

In conclusion, your committee express their unanimous opinion that the one important physical fact thus proved to exist, that *motion may be produced in solid bodies without material contact, by some hitherto unrecognised force operating within an undefined distance from the human organism, and beyond the range of muscular action,* should be subjected to further scientific examination, with a view to ascertain its true source, nature, and power.

The notes of the experiments made at each meeting of your sub-committee are appended to this report.

## ADDITIONAL EXPERIMENTS.

But although as a committee our work was ended, the phenomena we had witnessed, and of whose reality we were assured by the most conclusive evidence, could not but induce in the most thoughtful of the members various conjectures as to the nature and origin of the Force whose existence had thus been exhibited to them, and it is not surprising that wide differences of opinion should have prevailed among us as to its source. For my own part, I resolved to hold my judgment in suspense, and to continue the investigation with a view to learn, if possible, the causes of the phenomena I had so unexpectedly witnessed. Accordingly, the experiments were resumed under new conditions and with further tests.

It would be tedious and needless to describe fully each of these experiments. Those of the sub-committee are fully set forth in the appendix to the published report (a) of the Dialectical Society, to which the reader is referred. I will merely state briefly the most interesting results of these investigations, premising that all but three of them were made with *unpaid and unprofessional* Psychics.

1. The hand of the Psychic being held over it, a musical box upon the table, untouched, turned half round by four movements.

2. A sheet of paper was suspended by one corner from a pin which the Psychic held at the ends between the thumb and fingers, so that the hand could not touch the paper. Many taps, as if made with the point of a needle, were distinctly heard upon the paper.

3. The sounds frequently seemed to be directed by

---

(a) Report of the Committee of the London Dialectical Society, on the asserted Phenomena of Spiritualism, p. 407.

intelligence. They were made often in pursuance of and in answer to requests—as that so many blows should be struck, that the tappings should beat time to music, that they should be loud or soft, quick or slow.

4. So also, in like manner, the motions of the table, when untouched as well as when touched, were in exact accordance with requests, such as that it should tilt on this side or on that so many times. This was so frequent an occurrence that it was impossible to attribute it to accidental coincidence. So far from obedience being rare, as some scientists have conjectured, failure was the rare exception.

5. Occasionally the phenomena continued after the departure of the Psychic from the room, but in such cases they gradually diminished in power until they ceased entirely.

All the above phenomena were witnessed by the Investigation Committee of the Dialectical Society in the course of their experiments. The following experiments were witnessed by myself elsewhere:

6. The next experiment was with the same Psychic, in the house of Dr. Edmunds, with a dining-table of unusual weight and size. The same test, by turning the backs of the chairs to the table and the experimentalists kneeling upon them, produced the same results, but to a much greater extent than we had before witnessed. In that position of the entire party, a heavy dining-table moved six times—once over a space of eight inches at a swing. Then all the party holding hands stood in a circle round the table, at the distance from it first, of two feet, and then of

three feet, so that contact by any person present was physically impossible. In this position the table lurched four times, once over a space of *more than two feet*, and with great force. The extent of these movements without contact will be understood when I state that in the course of them *this ponderous table turned completely round*, that is to say, the end that was at the top of the room when the experiment began was at the bottom of the room when it concluded. The most remarkable part of this experiment was the finale. The table had been turned to within two feet of a complete reversal of its first position, and was standing out of square with the room. The party had broken up and were gathered in groups about the room. Suddenly the table was swung violently over the two feet of distance between its then position and its proper place, and set exactly square with the room, literally knocking down a lady who was standing in the way, in the act of putting on her shawl for departure. At that time *nobody was touching the table*, nor even within reach of it, except the young lady who was knocked down by it.

7. The next experiment was with another Psychic, in another place, but at the house of a personal friend, so that I have the best assurance that there could have been no such pre-arrangement of mechanism in the room as would have been necessary to produce the effects I describe.

It was a double drawing-room, in one of which was a table of considerable weight. The Psychic (a Lady who was *unpaid*, but known to be a Psychic), was taking tea in one room, and I had gone with three friends—one of whom had never before witnessed the phenomena—into the other 'room to look at some pictures. While we were thus engaged, very loud sounds, as of violent blows, came from a large loo table, which stood alone in the centre of the room—*nobody being near it.* We turned to look at the table, and untouched it tilted up almost to an angle of 45°, and continued in that position for nearly a minute. Then it fell back. Then it repeated the movement on the other side. None of us were standing within five feet of it at that time. The room was well lighted with gas. There was no cloth upon the table, and all beneath it was distinctly visible. Only four persons were in the room, and no one touched it, nor was near enough to touch it had he tried. The Psychic was six feet from it.

8. Alterations in the weight of tables and other furniture have been frequently exhibited. Bidding the table to be light, a finger lifted it ; the next moment, bidding it to be heavy, the entire force of the body was required to raise it from the floor. It was, however, suggested by myself and others who were engaged in the *scientific* investigation of the phenomena of Psychic Force, that possibly this change in the weight of the subject of the Force might be merely in our own sensations, and not an actual change in the gravity of the wood or the operation of any pressure upon it. To test this, a weighing machine was constructed with a hook to fix to the table, the index accurately marking the weight of whatever was attached to it. Applying this machine to the table and other bodies, we found that the change was really in them, and not sensational merely, as we had suspected. This simple experiment

was tried so often, and with so many precautions, as to establish it beyond doubt. The weights varied at every trial, but all proved the reality of the Force that was operating. One instance will suffice. Weighed by the machine, the normal weight of a table, raised from the floor 18 in. on one side, was 8lb.; desired to be light, the index fell to 5lb.; desired to be heavy, it advanced to *eighty-two* pounds; and these changes were instantaneous and repeated many times.

9. Not only is motion communicated to the table or other article of furniture where the Psychic is, but everything within some definite, though as yet undefined, distance from the Psychic appears to be subjected to the Force. The smaller furniture of the room is frequently attracted to the place at which the Psychic sits. Chairs far out of reach and untouched may be seen moving along the floor in a manner singularly resembling the motion that may be observed in pieces of steel attracted by a magnet, which rise a little, fall, move on, stop, until fully within the influence of the magnetic force, and then jump to the magnet with a sudden spring. The chairs that are so often seen to come across a room to the Psychic usually approach by irregular motions, gliding for a short space, stopping, moving, and so on, until fully within the influence, and then the last movement is by a rapid jump. Larger articles of furniture are attracted in like manner according to weight; chairs move easily the whole length of a large room, a sofa will advance 2ft. or 3ft. only. Plainly the Force is limited in power; it can move only a certain *weight;* bulk is no impediment to its exercise. Nor is this phenomenon at all dubious to

the spectator. It cannot be fanciful; it is not a delusion. However it may be done, *the fact* is indisputable that it *is* done. The chairs start from the wall against which they are placed; the sofa rolls forward; the smaller tables approach. This occurs in the light of gas, in the private room of any person who makes trial of it, is seen by all, and often gives inconvenient proof of the fact by encompassing the seated circle. At one experiment six drawing-room chairs were attracted from the other side of the room over distances ranging from 6ft. to 10ft., and thrust themselves against the circle; two large easy chairs advanced 3ft.; a large settee advanced about 2ft. No person was near either of them. In another experiment in my own lighted drawing-room, as the Psychic was entering the door with myself, no *other person being there*, an easy chair, of great weight, that was standing 14ft. from us, was suddenly lifted from the floor, and drawn to him with great rapidity, precisely as a huge magnet would attract a mass of iron.

## ARE THE SPECTATORS BIOLOGISED?

There yet remained one solution, often advanced, but always by those who have never witnessed the phenomena,—that the spectators are under the influence of electro-biology (whatever that may be), and imagine they see what the operator wishes them to see; that, precisely as the biologised patient believes, at the will of the operator, that his chair is on fire, so the persons about the Psychic, in obedience to the influence of *his* will, *suppose* that they see and hear what is, in fact, only a waking dream suggested by him.

Improbable as is this ingenious explanation of the phenomena described, it is not altogether impossible. We certainly believed ourselves to be very wide awake; the same things were seen and heard by all at the same moment; actual measurement showed changes in the position of the bodies moved; the vibration caused by the sounds we heard were distinct to the touch also. Nevertheless, we were most desirous to apply some *mechanical* test, which would preclude the possibility of this or any other mental delusion. There is no passion, prejudice, or capacity for self-delusion in wood and brass, and to that conclusive test it was determined to resort. Accordingly Mr. CROOKES, F.R.S., constructed the apparatus which he has described so fully, whereby not only could the existence of any Force be demonstrated by delicate tests, but the amount and direction of it measured with perfect accuracy.

Mr. HUGGINS, F.R.S., the astronomer and spectroscopist, as one practically skilled in the construction and working of the most delicate scientific apparatus, and myself as having great experience in the sifting and weighing of evidence, were invited to witness a trial of these experiments. The results have been given to the world in the *Quarterly Journal of Science,* and they completely establish the existence of a Force, operating within an undefined but not indefinite distance from certain persons having some unknown specialty of organization, and to which the appropriate name has been given of PSYCHIC Force, to distinguish it from MUSCULAR force; the latter operating only with, but the former without, actual personal contact.

## WHAT IS THE PSYCHIC FORCE?

A FORCE is visibly, palpably, audibly operating before us. It is manifest to three of our senses. *Can* all of these be deceived? Is it possible that the three senses of ten persons, seeing, hearing, and feeling the same thing at the same moment in the same manner, can be the dupes of a mere imagination? Were the motions we witnessed real or fanciful; were the sounds we heard actual or ideal? If what we saw and heard was not sufficient proof of the. *fact*, all evidence is worthless and truth is unattainable. On similar evidence a jury would instantly convict of murder and a judge would hang without hesitation. All the business of life is conducted in reliance upon less evidence of the same senses. If we are to reject the testimony of such experiments as these, we must reject all testimony of the eye, the ear, and the touch. Three-fourths of the sciences are based upon experiments infinitely more open to doubt and question than those which establish the existence of the Force, whatever it may be, that moves and makes audible sounds on heavy bodies without physical contact or connection. Its existence is demonstrated by evidence as certain and perfect as that which proves the existence of electricity, magnetism, and other invisible and intangible forces of nature. It was impossible for us, with such evidence, repeated

thirty-eight times, under various te: u and divers conditions, to do other than acknowledge *the existence* of
the Force we had thought by our experiments to dis-
prove, although we failed to come to any satisfactory
conclusion with respect to the *souree* and *nature* of that
Force. Upon these points very wide differences of
opinion prevailed, some deeming it to be a spiritual
presence, others, and the scientific observers especially,
coinciding with my own conviction that it is a purely
physical force, proceeding in some as yet untraced manner from the nerve organization—probably the nerve
atmosphere which Dr. Richardson contends is envelop-
ing all of us,—extended in Psychics to an abnormal
distance from the extremities of the nerves, and directed by the same intelligence that governs the action
of the nerves themselves; the motive power being frequently that unconscious action of the brain which Dr.
Carpenter has investigated with so much ability and
success, to which he has given the name of "Unconscious Cerebration," and for asserting which he has been
so mercilessly accused of gullibility by his brother
Scientists.

But it will be just to state fairly the contention on
either side among those who acknowledge the existence
of the Force but differ in opinion as to its origin.

The most numerous, though not the most scientific,
section are they who, unable to explain the phenomena
upon the instant, have adopted the time-honoured practice of solving a scientific problem by the easy process
of assigning it to the convenient region of the supernatural. As it ever was, so it is now. Each one of
Nature's Forces has in its turn been attributed to angels

or demons, before Science condescended to recognise its facts and give them a place in its own domain. As soon as the fact is seized, stripped of all that fancy has thrown about it, investigated, measured, and found to fit, as all facts do, with the natural order of things, that fact has instantly ceased to be the subject of superstition.

So it will be with the Psychic Force. When recognised by Science as one of the natural forces, it will speedily cease to be a superstition itself or the parent of superstition. All honour to the man who has had the courage to grapple with it and drag it out of the possession of Superstition into the domain of Science.

Wherefore do we call it *Psychic* Force? To distinguish it from *Muscular* Force.

Distinctly associated with the human organisation, it may be, probably it is, that it exists in all human beings in greater or less degree; but so far the evidence is, that it is possessed to an extraordinary extent by certain persons, to whom the appropriate name of *Psychics* is proposed to be given. It is not exhibited save within an undefined, but still limited, circle about a Psychic. It varies from day to day, from hour to hour, almost from minute to minute, according to the nervous condition of the Psychic. It issues in pulsations, as was plainly manifested in the experiments made with Mr. Crookes's mechanism, and minutely described in the *Quarterly Journal of Science.* Whatever affects the Psychic instantly affects the Force. It comes with him and goes with him. All the conditions, more fully to be set out hereafter, point directly to the Psychic as the source of it.

And that is the conclusion of the scientific section of the investigators, with few exceptions.

On the other hand, the majority of the unscientific relieve their minds from the disagreeable condition of doubt by assuming the Force to be spiritual. This is so easy a solution of every problem in nature we are unable to solve at once, that it has ever been the favourite means of accounting for the unaccountable.

## The Theory of Spiritualism.

The " Spiritualists," for that is the name they have assumed in accordance with their theory, have exercised considerable ingenuity in moulding that theory to the facts. Their creed, as I gather it from the most intelligent of its votaries, may be thus briefly described :—

Man, they say, is composed of body, mind, and spirit. A blow will extinguish the mind, and the body inhabited by the spirit may continue to live. When the body dies, the spirit which occupied it in life passes into a new existence, in which, as it was here, it is surrounded by conditions adapted to its structure as a being which by earthly senses is deemed immaterial because impalpable to them, but which is really very refined matter. Into this new existence it passes precisely as it left the present life, taking with it the mental, but not the bodily, characteristics it had on earth, so far as these are adapted to the altered conditions of that new existence. The intellect is enlarged to the extent only of the increased power of obtaining intelligence necessarily resulting from exemption from the laws of gravitation and the conditions of time and space that limit the powers of the spirit while it is in the flesh.

The reason, say the Spiritualists, why we are not always conscious of the presence of the spirits that are thronging everywhere about us is that our senses are constructed to perceive only the coarse material of this earth, and therefore we cannot perceive the refined matter of which a spirit is composed. If a spirit touches us, we can no more feel the touch than we can *feel* the particles of musk that another sense tells us are filling the room. The disembodied spirit has no means of communication with us in ordinary circumstances, because its substance is not perceptible by our senses.

A Psychic (or Medium, as the Spiritualists call him) is a person possessing an abnormal amount of animal magnetism (which is the name *they* give to what *we* call the Psychic Force). This is something that proceeds from the human body—matter of some kind projected from the whole or part of the structure, and, like the other forces of nature, is perceptible to our senses only when it meets with some obstacle. All possess it, more or less. The medium has it more, and thus attracts it from those with whom he is in communication. When this affluent substance is sufficiently abundant, the spirits, which are always about us, are enabled to use it as a medium of communication between themselves and human beings. They have power to seize and shape it into a substance palpable to our senses. Hence the need for the presence of a medium. Hence the uncertainty of the manifestations. Hence the continual fluctuations of the magnetic material, according to external conditions of health, atmosphere, temperature, and other influences.

A spirit, say the Spiritualists, of necessity can manifest itself to our senses only by assuming a substance sufficiently solid to make an impression upon some one of them. We might be surrounded by spirits and yet be utterly unconscious of their presence. The air may be so thronged with them that we could never lift an arm without touching or passing through a spirit, and yet we might live and die in perfect ignorance of their presence, because our senses are incapable of perceiving the impressions made by matter more refined than that which they are constructed to perceive.

In this Spiritualist creed there is nothing absolutely *impossible.* It may be that, as Milton sings:

Millions of spiritual creatures walk the earth,
Unseen both when we wake and when we sleep.

As Lord Lytton says, seeing how life teems in all the visible creation, it may be a not unreasonable presumption that the vast interspaces between the worlds are not altogether void of life, and it is conceivable that spirit, in its infinite immateriality, may find there a dwelling-place.

But, however ingenious this creed may be, the question is, if it be not purely speculative—a merely fanciful creation, unsupported by any solid *facts?* True, that it explains all the phenomena of Psychism, but so it would explain every other problem in science—and it has, in fact, been invoked for that purpose in all ages and countries. All of the many marvels of science were sought to be explained at first by the easy process of referring them to supernatural (or spirit) power, until sober-minded men investigated them, and proved them to be purely natural, and then they ceased to be the subjects of wonder and the basis of superstition.

So it will be with the speculations of Spiritualism. Touched by Science its visions will vanish, and the facts that lie at the bottom of it will become a solid and invaluable addition to our knowledge of the physiology and psychology of Man.

### THE SCIENTIFIC THEORY OF PSYCHIC FORCE.

On the other hand, the scientific theory of the Psychic Force whose existence may now be deemed to be demonstrated, may be shortly stated thus:—

There is a Force proceeding from, or directly associated with, the human organisation, which, in certain persons and under certain conditions, can cause motion in heavy bodies, and produce audible and palpable sounds in such bodies, without muscular contact or any material connection between any person present and the heavy body so moved or on which the sounds are produced.

This Force appears to be frequently directed by some intelligence.

For the reasons presently to be specified, we conclude that this Force is generated in certain persons of peculiar nervous organisation in sufficient power to operate beyond bodily contact. To these persons the Spiritualists have given the name of "mediums," on the assumption that they are the means of communication between disembodied spirits and the living; but they who, with myself, dispute the theory of Spiritualism, have given to those persons the more appropriate name of *Psychics*.

There can be little doubt that the Force is possessed by every human being,—that it is a necessary condition of the living nerve, if, indeed, it be not the vital force itself; but that it is possessed by Psychics in extraordinary degree. In ordinary persons it ceases to operate at or near the extremities of the nerves; in Psychics it flows beyond them in waves of varying volume and power. Mr. Crookes, indeed, has recently constructed an instrument of extreme delicacy, which seems to indicate the existence of the Psychic Force more or less in every person with whom he has made trial of it.

The existence of such a Force is asserted by Dr. Richardson, in a recent article in the *Popular Science Review*, in which he contends that there is a nerve fluid (or ether), with which the nerves are enveloped, and by whose help it is that the motion of their molecules communicates sensations and transmits the commands of the will. This nerve ether is, he thinks, no other than the vital force. It extends with all of us somewhat beyond the extremities of the nerve structure, and even beyond the surface of·the body, encompassing us wholly with an envelope of nerve atmosphere, which varies in its depth and intensity in various persons. This, he contends, will solve many difficult problems in Psychology and throw a new light on many obscurities in Physiology and Mental Philosophy.

If Dr. Richardson be confirmed in this discovery, there can be little doubt that the Psychic Force is that nerve ether or nerve atmosphere.

But, say the Spiritualists, your Psychic Force is directed by some intelligence. How is *that* to be accounted for? Whence and what is that intelligence? Unless you can show that it proceeds from the Psychic, or some person present, you *must* conclude that it is the

product of some other being, and as no other being is
visibly present that being must be a spirit.

To this argument of the Spiritualists, urged in a
tone of triumph, the advocates of a Psychic Force have
an answer, which appears to be complete.

We contend that the intelligence that directs the Psychic Force is the intelligence of the Psychic and no other.
The reasons for such a conclusion will be set forth
presently and will be admitted by the impartial to be
overwhelming. All the conditions requisite to the
production and exercise of the Force are consistent
with its origin in and direction by the Psychic and
inconsistent with any conceivable action of the disembodied spirits of the dead.

But for the manner in which the force may be
governed I must turn to Dr. Carpenter; as for its source
I have referred to the authority of Dr. Richardson.

The explanation will be found in Dr. Carpenter's
theory of "unconscious cerebration," or, in less learned
language, the capacity of the brain, under certain conditions, to work, not only without the will, but without
the consciousness, of the individual. A familiar instance of this is seen in the case of a person stunned.
He will walk, talk, return to his home, undress, go to
bed, although consciousness is annihilated, and when
he "recovers his senses" as it is called, he has no
memory of anything, not even of time, from the
moment when the blow was received to the moment of
consciousness revived. Another instance is the frequent
one of somnambulism, natural and artificial, in both of
which states the brain acts perfectly and often more
powerfully than in the normal state, while consciousness

is suspended. Numerous instances are collected by Dr. Carpenter, who attributes to this curious condition most of the phenomena of mesmerism, electro-biology, and other hitherto mysterious mental states which scientific men, unable to explain, have contented themselves with denying or ignoring, and unreflecting persons have attributed to supernatural influences, as the solution nearest at hand. But if this be the true cause, nothing is more simple and obvious than the application of it to the facts that have so long perplexed physiologists and mental philosophers, and for accepting which as *facts* (though they could not explain them) so many honest observers have been called dupes or knaves.

This is probably the Intelligence that directs the Psychic Force. It is the brain of the Psychic in that condition of "unconscious cerebration" of which Dr. Carpenter has demonstrated the existence, and which he has dared to maintain in defiance of the accusations of being gullible made by his scientific brethren, always jealous of those who claim the honour of a new discovery.

The Scientific theory, then, which I venture to oppose to the Spiritualist theory of phenomena, whose existence is demonstrated by evidence as conclusive as any that establishes the other facts of Science, is that the Force whose operations are seen in the motion of heavy bodies when untouched and heard in the audible and palpable sounds that come from them, is the Force which Dr. Richardson contends to be always existing in the nerve system, and that the Intelligence which as certainly often directs that Force is the "Unconscious Cerebration" of Dr. Carpenter.

### THE ARGUMENT FOR THE PSYCHIC THEORY.

I now propose to set forth the facts that appear to me
to give consistent support to the *Scientific* theory
thus stated, and to be entirely inconsistent with the
Spiritualist theory. These are—

I. The necessity for the presence of a human being
having some unascertained peculiarity of constitution,
whom the Spiritualists call " a Medium," but to whom
the Scientists have preferred to give the more scientific
title of " a Psychic."

II. A Psychic is a person possessing no known
superiority of mind or body. He differs in no perceptible manner from other persons. The faculty is not
associated with any special intelligence or virtue, nor
with any condition of health or of disease, nor with
any sex, age, complexion, or form. A child is usually
a more powerful Psychic than a man. The possessor
of the Psychic Force has no consciousness of its
existence in himself until an accident discovers it.

III. The Psychic is an unconscious agent. He can
neither command nor control the Force. It does not
come nor depart at his will. He has no more knowledge of its presence than has any of the spectators.

IV. Psychic Force is always exhibited within a
limited range from the person of the Psychic. Its
power appears to decline according to distance, but at
what ratio remains to be determined. It is, however,
certain that usually, if not always, it operates far beyond the reach of his muscular powers.

V. It is sometimes, but rarely, exhibited when the
Psychic is alone. As a rule, the presence of other persons promotes the operations of the Force.

VI. For this purpose such other persons must be within the range of the Force proceeding from the Psychic.

VII. It is found to be advantageous, though by no means necessary, that the persons present with the Psychic should form a circle after the manner of the electric chain. The Force is promoted by the joining of hands, but almost the same effect is produced by laying the hands on a table or on any other solid body, such body appearing to be in the nature of a conductor, and possibly of a collector, of the Force.

VIII. The persons forming the chain may be of any age, sex, intelligence, or virtue. Scepticism *in no way* impedes the manifestation of the Force. But there are certain persons whose presence, from some cause not yet ascertained, operates precisely as does the interposition of a non-conducting substance in the electric chain. They impede the flow of the Force, but how or why we are wholly ignorant. This, however, is of unfrequent occurrence, and is no way connected with belief or disbelief. Believers are non-conductors equally with others.

IX. It is not known how the Psychic Force is affected by the presence of such a person. One probable conjecture is that all human beings possess Psychic Force in a greater or less degree, and that the greater Force of the Psychic attracts to itself the lesser Psychic Force of the persons with whom he is sitting, the use of the circle or chain being to collect and convey the Psychic Force of the whole party.

X. The Force is materially affected by the conditions attendant on the formation of the circle. Whatever tends to bring all the minds present into harmonious action obviously promotes the action of the Force. General conversation on a common topic, prayer, recitation, and, above all, music, are marked and universal in their effect of increasing the flow and power of the Force. On the contrary, whatever directs the various minds in the circle into diverse action, as talking on different matters, or on themes creating discordant opinion or exciting rival emotions, operates invariably to weaken, and often to extinguish, the Force during the continuance of such diversity of mental action: and it is revived on recourse to music, or whatever has the effect of restoring harmonious brain action.

*Note.*—If there be, as many physiologists contend, a stream of waves of vital force incessantly thrown off by the nerve centres, and to which the name of "brain wave" has been given, it is readily intelligible how discordant discussion should dissipate the Psychic Force and music promote it. When all the brains present are working in harmony, the waves thrown off are synchronous, and all swell the flow of the stream through the conductor to the attracting Force of the Psychic. But if the actions of the brains are discordant, the brain waves, by a well known law, fall foul of each other, and being thus partially neutralized, the flow of the stream is diminished, and even destroyed.

XI. The condition of the Psychic is found largely to affect the exhibition of the Force. Its presence and power are dependent upon the state of mind and of body in the Psychic, and vary from time to time with that state. Often a headache will destroy it; a cup of tea, that revives the nerve energy, revives also the Psychic Force. The state of the atmosphere visibly influences it. Accordingly as it is wet or dry, cold or hot, so is the power lesser or greater. But the state of

the weather does not affect all Psychics alike.    That
which gives power to some takes it away from others.
I know two powerful Psychics in private life, in one of
whom the force is at zero in hot and moist weather,
vigorous in cold and dry weather; in the other, it is
powerful in the former, almost powerless in the latter.
But in both the weather that thus differently affects
their Psychic Force affects also their general health.

XII. The degree of the Force varies continually
during the experiments, not merely from hour to hour,
but almost from minute to minute.    The opening of a
door will sometimes produce an immediate flow of it;
the change of two or three degrees of temperature will
raise or depress it.    In fact, whatever affects the
Psychic personally, and to a less extent the persons
with him, affects the power of the Force.

XIII. The communications made by the intelligence
that undoubtedly often directs the Force are character-
istic of the Psychic; as he is so they are.    The language, and even spelling, are such as he uses; the
ideas are such as he would be likely to possess—neither
better nor worse.    If he were to communicate avowed-
ly with his own bodily organs, it would be done in
precisely the same manner.    Thus the communications
in the presence of an English Psychic are in English
phrase, of a Scotch Psychic in Scotticisms, of a pro-
vincial in his own provincialisms, of a Frenchman in
French.    The *ideas* conveyed are those of the Psychic.
If he is intellectual so are the communications.    If vul-
gar or uneducated so are they.    Their religious tone
varies with the faith of the Psychic.    In the presence
of a Methodist Psychic, the communications are Meth-

odistical; of a Roman Catholic, decidedly Papistical; with a Unitarian, free-thinking views prevail. If the Psychic cannot spell, the communications are faulty in the spelling; if the Psychic is ignorant of grammar, the defect is seen in the sentences spelled by the Force. If the Psychic is ill-informed on matters of fact, as in science, and such like, the alleged spirit messages exhibit the same errors, and if the communication has relation to a future state, the descriptions given of that sphere of existence are in strict accordance with the notions which such a person as the Psychic might be expected to entertain of it.

*Note.*—I am aware that the answer of the Spiritualists to this patent objection is the ingenious one, that when the spirit quits its mortal tenement, it carries with it all the mental qualities and faculties it possessed here—the same knowledge and no other, and that in its new sphere of existence it can obtain further intelligence only by the same process of instruction as in this world. Hence its inability to give any new knowledge. It is further asserted that we who are in the flesh are attended only by spirits who sympathize with our own mental condition, and hence the resemblances I have stated between their communications and the mental condition of the Psychic. But the reader will say if this is not more like a clever theory, invented to explain the facts, than the natural deduction from the facts themselves. It appears to me to be incredible that the soul, having passed from this world into a new stage of existence, with powers enlarged to, at least, the extent necessarily consequent upon the condition of immateriality, and its resulting exemption from the laws of gravitation, and from time and space as conceived by the material brain, should not be better informed than we who are in the flesh can be as to which of many religions is the true one. Yet do we find different communications, equally alleged to be spiritual, differing essentially as to what is the truth, each declaring with the same positiveness that its own creed is the only true one, and that creed being always the creed of the Psychic.

XIV. The Force exhibits itself in pulsations or undulations. It is never steadily continuous. Moreover it is rhythmical in its exhibitions, coming at equal intervals. The rappings are very regular; the motions of heavy bodies observe perfect time. The tremors of the table, of the chair, of the floor of the room, are as rapid and as regular as the waves of light or sound. When a table or a chair rises from the floor, it does not ascend with a jerk, as if pushed up, nor descend with a thump, as if a sustaining hand had been removed from it. It soars and sinks like a balloon, precisely as if it had been released from the force of gravity, and was going upward by its own levity. The difference of the sensation between the operation of the Psychic Force and of muscular force is in this particular so manifest as to be palpable instantly to everybody who witnesses it. When solid bodies are seen to rise without contact, the motion is very peculiar and always the same. They do not dart straight up, like a balloon, but with a swinging motion, much like that of a pendulum. They do not remain still when at the highest ascent, but quiver with immense rapidity or continue the pendulous motion, and return with an irregular hesitating descent, after the manner of a parachute. In Mr. CROOKES's experiments with the mechanical board, this pulsatory motion was very distinctly marked, the indicator attached to the balance showing an incessant tremulous up and down movement throughout the operation of the Force, such movement being manifestly the flow of the Force in synchronous waves varying in intensity.

XV. The Force is materially influenced by the electric and magnetic conditions of the atmosphere and of surrounding bodies; by heat and cold, by moisture and dryness, and still more by the nervous condition of the persons present, and especially of the Psychic.

*Note.*—These conditions are precisely such as would be likely to affect the flow of the Force from the Psychic, but difficult to assert as being likely to affect disembodied spirits. It cannot be said to be impossible, but it is certainly highly improbable that spirits, according to any reasonable conception of their nature, could be impeded in their action by a shower of rain, a close room, the order in which people sit, the headache of one person and the toothache of another. But these incidents would necessarily affect a Psychic Force.

XVI. The Force is not exhibited immediately, save in rare instances. There is an interval of more or less duration, frequently above half an hour, before any symptoms of its presence are shown. Let a stethoscope be then applied to the table, and faint creakings are audible *in the body*, not at the surface, of the wood, as if a pin was striking its fibres. The sounds grow louder by degrees, and occasionally are so loud as to be audible in distant rooms, and they proceed from the wall, the ceiling, and pieces of furniture far beyond the reach of the Psychic, as well as from the table at which the party is seated. Wherever heard they appear to proceed from within, rather than from the surface. The vibrations are distinctly felt by the hand, insomuch that a deaf person can usually discover the blows and their communications as readily as they who have the use of their ears. The motions also grow in vigour; they begin with a faint tremor, then a violent shaking of the entire fabric; then tiltings, now on this side, now on that, and then rising from the ground, all which conditions indicate the operation of a purely mundane

force. The process is similar to that seen in the gathering of the electric force ; it must be accumulated before
it becomes powerful, or even sensible to us—at least,
there is waiting for an indefinite time, and then a slow
but steady growth of the Force, and ultimately the
Psychic becomes exhausted by the process.

XVII. Anything that strongly diverts the mind of
the Psychic or the thoughts of the persons present
always diminishes the Force.

XVIII. The presence of a sceptic is no obstacle to
the exhibition of the Force. It is otherwise with positive antagonism. By disturbing the mind of the Psychic, and perhaps of others, it probably destroys that
harmonious action of the brain which appears to be
essential to the operation of the Psychic Force.

*Note.*—All of the above conditions are wholly *in*consistent with
the spiritual theory, and entirely consistent with the physical
theory, of the origin of this Force.

XIX. So far as I have found in my own experiments, and by the reported experience of others, it appears that the intelligence of the communications is
measured by the intelligence of the Psychic. Nothing
is conveyed by them that is not in the mind of the
Psychic or of some person present.

XX. There is nothing in the character or substance
of the communications indicating an intelligence higher
than our own, or a larger knowledge. They are often
useless and purposeless ; they are rarely absolute nonsense ; but as rarely do they exhibit anything beyond
ordinary intelligence. They consist mainly of moral
platitudes; both the thoughts and the language reflect
precisely the thoughts and language of the Psychic.

XXI. Not unfrequently the communications are false in point of fact. They are often tentative, as if the directing intelligence had an imperfect perception of the object or subject, or as if it were guessing rather than knowing the answer to be given.

XXII. The descriptions of the future life are precisely such as the Psychic would form. By a child Psychic they are painted according to a child's notion of heaven ; and when the Psychic is a man or a woman, they are described in accordance with the particular conceptions of a heaven entertained by that Psychic.

*Note.*—These differences as to the process of death and the conditions of a future life prove that the descriptions do not proceed from any intelligence actually acquainted with them, and therefore not from the spirits of the dead.

XXIII. The movements of solid bodies, as previously described, when made without contact, are, if not always, almost always *towards* the Psychic : and, as if by some attractive force in him, the chairs and other furniture that appear to move spontaneously from their places, at whatever distance from the Psychic, invariably advance towards him in a direct line, if some obstacle is not interposed. When a chair, for instance, comes to the side of the table that is opposite to him, it is because the table stands in the path of a straight line from the spot whence it started to the Psychic.

*Note.*—I am informed that this attraction *to* the Psychic is not always seen, but that sometimes, though rarely, solid bodies appear to be repelled, and to move *from* him. I am narrating only my own experiments, and I have never witnessed an instance of a repulsive motion. Every spontaneous movement of furniture, within my own observation, has been in a direction *towards* the Psychic. What can raise a stronger presumption than this, that the attractive force is in the Psychic? Indeed, the Spiritualists find themselves compelled to admit the existence of a Psychic Force (calling it magnetic), but they account for the facts stated above by the ingenious but wholly conjectural explanation that the disembodied spirits, by whom the motions, sounds, and communications are believed by them to be made, gather up and employ the magnetism of the Psychic as the material by which they are enabled to manifest themselves to mortal senses, and that thence arises the remarkable similarity which the acts done, and the communications made, invariably bear to the mental character and intelligence of the Psychic.

Such being some of the principal conditions that I have noted as attending the manifestations of the Psychic Force, what are the conclusions to which they point?

First, that the Psychic Force itself proceeds from, or in some unknown manner is associated with, the human organisation.

Second, that it is controlled and directed by the intelligence of the Psychic.

The manner in which this is effected is undiscovered, because as yet it has not been examined scientifically.

That it is the result of an *unconscious* action of the brain, the ganglion, or the nerves, will probably be deemed by those who have closely noted the phenomena to be sufficiently established. The attention of the Psychic does not require to be fixed upon what is going on. Answers are given to questions while the Psychic is conversing on other subjects, and even when the questions are put so faintly that he could not hear them had he been listening instead of talking.

And not only are all of these ascertained conditions consistent with the *scientific* conclusion, that the Force both proceeds from, and is directed by the intelligence of, the Psychic, but they are inconsistent with the Spiritualist theory, that they are the doings of the disembodied spirits of the dead. All is precisely as might be anticipated of the Psychic that he would act and speak in such case; nothing is done or communicated in any fashion such as might reasonably be supposed that a disembodied spirit would do or say.

In such circumstances, the course prescribed alike by Science and common sense is to accept the near and natural solution in preference to the distant and the supernatural. There is a Force visibly, audibly, and palpably at work, and it is undoubtedly directed by intelligence. Whence does it come? Either from one or more or all of the persons present, or from some invisible being. If all the conditions attending the operations of the Force are consistent with the former and inconsistent with the latter hypothesis, science, reason, and common sense direct us to prefer the former—to accept the theory of Psychism in preference to the theory of Spiritualism.

## CHARACTERISTICS OF THE FORCE.

THE term *Psychic Force* has been employed to describe the power or influence that either proceeds from or is intimately associated with the human organisation, not as being a perfect name for it, but for want of a fitter one. We call it *a Force* because many of the phenomena present the results of force. But it must not therefore be taken as an affirmation on the part of those who, with myself, assert the theory of its human origin, and contend that it falls within the proper domain of science, that it necessarily resembles the other powers in nature to which science has given the name of "forces." The notion of the forces of heat, light, magnetism, electricity, galvanism (be they the same or many), is that of particles in motion, making themselves perceptible to our senses when they strike against some opposing matter, though that is very difficult to comprehend, seeing that magnetism, like Psychic Force, operates, although a solid body is interposed between the magnet and the object it attracts. But it does not follow that in this particular Psychic Force should resemble those other forces. We call it a force for convenience, and for lack of a better term; but it is doubtful if, strictly speaking, it be a *force*—if it be not more in the nature of an *influence* than of motion of particles projected and impinging on other bodies and by the impact causing motions and sounds on the bodies struck. The subject is extremely obscure, very little endeavour having been made to examine it patiently, with experiments and tests guided by sagacity, as Science has investigated other phenomena, and with a sincere desire to learn the very truth, however disturbing that truth may be to accepted principles and opinions.

With this protest against a possible misunderstanding of our meaning when we talk of Psychic Force, I ask a short consideration of its foremost characteristics.

I. The force, or influence, comes in waves that are in rapid motion, rising and falling continually. The waves are generally synchronous, but of uneven magnitude. They are more or less tremulous to the perceptive sense. The things moved by it, whatever they may be, with rare exceptions *quiver*, in this particular differing in a very marked manner from muscular force, which is exercised either by sudden impact in the shape of a push or blow or by steady pressure. This difference in the character of Psychic Force at once distinguishes it from muscular force, and is of itself satisfactory proof that the phenomena are not the result of muscular action, either designed or unconscious.

II. In another respect the Psychic Force operates upon the bodies subjected to it in a manner altogether unlike muscular force. It is neither a blow, a push, nor a pressure. If the subject of the experiment be a table, for instance, the sounds are not upon the surface, as if something had struck the wood, but as if they were produced in the fibrous centre of the slab. The vibration is more palpable to the touch than when a blow of equal loudness is made upon the table. The

sound differs much from that produced by the finger or
by any instrument of wood or metal, insomuch that a
very brief experience suffices to enable the ear instantly
to discover the difference between artificial sounds and
the true sound of the Psychic Force.

So it is with motions of solid bodies caused by the
Psychic Force. They have a special character. In
addition to the curious tremulousness or quivering that
attends these motions, they appear to be caused by
power exercised in a manner differing widely from
that of muscular action. An arm, for instance, applies
its force to one part of the subject only, and by no contrivance can extend that force equally over the whole
body. To refer again to the familiar instance of a table.
Muscular force, as of an arm, might raise or depress the
table on the side at which it is used—by application
above, it would be depressed; by application below,
it would be raised—but only at the point of contact;
and the foot applied to the leg of the table might lift it
on that side, but could not possibly depress it. The table
could not be raised entirely from the floor by any one
or more persons applying muscular pressure on one side
only, because of the inability to diffuse muscular force
equally throughout the entire body to be moved. A
table could be raised from the floor, preserving its hori-
zontal position, only by the application of the equal
muscular force of two persons, at the least, standing on
opposite sides. This is another proof that Psychic
Force is not muscular force, for scarcely an experiment
can be tried with a Psychic without motions of the
table being produced on the side of the table *opposite*
to that at which he is seated, and in a position which

makes the application of muscular force by him to that part of the table a sheer impossibility.

III. The Psychic Force appears to diffuse itself over the entire of the body to which it is applied, and to exercise itself in any part of that body with equal power and facility. The sides of the table opposite to the Psychic, far out of reach of muscular contact by him, are raised or depressed, and the sounds proceed from those parts quite as frequently and as vigorously as at the side of the table at which he is sitting, or within the reach of his muscular powers.

IV. The Psychic Force, unlike muscular force, does not appear to operate by pressure; it is more in the nature of diffusion and inflation; it is apparently a Force the material of which is wholly unknown to us. The bodies moved by it are not moved by a jerk, or by upward or downward continuous pressure applied to one portion of the subject only; the Psychic Force seems to diffuse itself through the whole substance of the thing moved. Thus, if it be a table, it is raised, not as by a force applied below, but as if by the levitation of the material of which it is composed. When it rises from the floor it mounts like a balloon. If the hand is pressed upon it in its ascent, instead of depressing it on that side and feeling a counter-pressure of resistance in some special part of it, the sensation to the touch is that of a floating body rising because it is lighter than the air: a sensation that will be at once recognised by those who have ever amused themselves with toy balloons. It hovers in the air like a *floating*, not like a *lifted*, body, and it descends generally with more or less of a pendulous motion, as in a descending balloon, or a parachute. It never *falls* down like a solid mass.

V. From these characteristics of the action of Psychic Force, I am inclined to the conjecture (for as yet it is little more), that it is a force antagonistic to gravitation, or in some unknown manner exempt from the influence of gravitation, or at least that it operates to counteract the force of gravitation on the bodies in which it is diffused.

VI. This conjecture as to the nature of the Psychic Force appears to derive some confirmation from the process required for its exhibition. Muscular force needs no preparation for its exercise. An arm or a foot can be raised and will apply the same amount of force in an instant as in an hour. It cannot be accumulated in any body. The continued pressure of the hands upon a table does not increase the amount of muscular force applied to the table. That which enters at the point of contact is absorbed by the force of gravitation as fast as it is evolved, and at the end of half-an-hour the table cannot be moved more easily than at the end of a minute.

But the Psychic Force is evidently capable of accumulation. It grows by slow degrees. A lapse of time, varying according to many conditions not yet examined, is requisite before a sufficiency of it is infused into the subject to produce any perceptible effect. First come delicate sounds, audible only by help of a stethoscope; then these grow louder, and can be heard by the ear and felt by the hand; and then come the motions that no person who has once witnessed them can either imagine or mistake. But all this is mani-

festly the evidence of an accumulation of force, as
electricity is accumulated in a battery, or magnetism
in a coil; and the sitting with the hands upon the
table is the process of charging it (if I may use the
term) with the Psychic Force, which all human beings
possess in a greater or lesser degree, but which the
Psychic possesses in an abnormal degree, combined
with the power of directing it, when so accumulated,
in some manner as yet unknown, but which it should
be the business of Science to discover.

## CONCLUSION.

FROM the above experiments it is not unreasonable that they who witnessed them should have concluded—

I. That there is a Force other than the Forces of Nature hitherto recognised. But whether it is the one Force which is said to change merely its form according to the substance in which it is exhibited, or a Force entirely distinct from the known Physical Forces, and subject to other laws associated with vitality, there is not as yet sufficient evidence to determine.

II. That this Force produces positive sounds and motions in solid bodies brought within the radius of its influence.

III. That this Force is found to operate at an undefined, but not indefinite, distance from the human body.

IV. That it is developed (so as to be perceptible to the senses by its effects) in certain persons only, to whom the name of Psychics has been given.

V. That Psychics are not distinguished from other persons by any perceptible peculiarity of mental or bodily organisation. They are of either sex, of all ages, of all degrees of intelligence, of varying physical powers, of all degrees of bodily health, of all countries and races.

VI. That there is some, but not sufficient, evidence,

that the power of a Psychic is a special faculty (such as is a genius for music, poetry, &c.) and that it is often inherited.

VII. That it is probable (but not yet proved), that this Force proceeds from, or is intimately associated with, the nerve organisation, and is possessed by all human beings in a greater or less degree, but in their ordinary conditions producing no external effects perceptible by the senses; that when possessed to an extraordinary extent, this Force is projected beyond the body, and causes motions and sounds in the objects permeated by it, or upon which it impinges.

VIII. That there is some, but not yet sufficient, evidence, that Psychic Force, and what physiologists have termed "vital force," and Dr. Richardson the "nerve ether," are identical.

IX. That in some manner, as yet not investigated and therefore not ascertained, a concurrence of the Psychic Forces of several persons promotes the activity of the Force exhibited by the Psychic.

X. That it is as yet undetermined whether it is the possession of Psychic Force in a rare degree that makes itself perceptible by its operation upon solid bodies, or if a Psychic is only a person who has not in himself a greater amount of the Force than others, but who possesses the power of attracting the combined Psychic Forces of the persons who are within a certain undefined radius from himself.

XI. That the Psychic Force is controlled and directed by the intelligence of the Psychic. That this intelligence frequently acts without consciousness by the Psychic. But if such action is that of the brain, or of an individuality distinct from the brain and incorporeal, there is as yet no sufficient evidence.

XII. That the condition of the Psychic during such unconscious direction of the Force is generally similar to, if not identical with, that of the somnambulist, whose intelligent acts are the result of unconscious action of the brain, which not only dreams, but causes the patient to act the dream.

These are the results, concisely stated, obtained to the present time, of a scientific investigation into Psychic Force. It will be seen that they are, as from the recency of the procurement of *proofs* of the existence of the Force might have been surmised, as yet very imperfect. A few facts have been ascertained, but many more are yet in a dubious stage, awaiting further examination. The conditions under which the Psychic Force exists and is evolved and directed have been insufficiently examined, and there are numerous points in the wide field thus open to investigators to which their attention may be advantageously directed. I venture to state a few of these, in the hope that they will stimulate some readers to a course of experiment and test, with a view to obtain satisfactory solutions.

I. What are the precise measured distances from the Psychic to which the Psychic Force is found to extend ?

II. Does the Force diminish according to distance from the Psychic, and if so, in what ratio ?

III. What relationship do heat, moisture, electricity, and terrestrial magnetism severally bear to the amount of the Force exhibited ?

IV. To what extent is the Force affected by the num-ber of persons forming the chain?

V. Is there any, and how much, increase in the Force by the formation of a chain of nerve organizations, and in what degree by extension of the chain? Is the effect the same if the same persons are merely grouped to-gether near to the Psychic without forming a circle or in any manner uniting the Psychic Force possessed by each person, except by the common link of the floor on which they stand?

VI. Is the concentration or direction of the Force affected to any extent by the material of which is form-ed the table or other body used as a conductor or col-lector of the Force? Is metal more or less favourable to the exhibition of the Force than wood; and is one kind of wood more favourable than another kind?

VII. Does any advantage accrue in fact from actual contact of the persons present: and does not the table or other conductor employed equally serve for conduct-ing or collecting the Force?

VIII. By what process is it that the unconscious action of the brain, asserted by Dr. Carpenter, directs the Psychic Force to intelligent purposes?

I shall esteem it an obligation if any reader pursuing this interesting and most important investigation into the nature and operations of Psychic Force will com-municate to me the results of his experiments; for it is only by a large accumulation of facts, and a multitude of observations, made under a variety of conditions, that this branch of the science of Psychology can be ad-vanced. Careful note should be taken of all trials, and whatever is capable of actual measurement should be determined by rule or by scales.

, Let it once be recognised that this is a subject for Science, and not a mere structure of imagination nor a superstition erected upon a basis of fact, and there will be an end to the strange aversion now felt to the examination of phenomena which, if established, must throw a blaze of light on many of the obscurities of Physiology and mysteries of medicine.

Brought within the domain of Science, the facts recognised, examined, and traced to their sources, so much as is true will be added to the store of knowledge; so much as is false, or which fancy may have erected upon the facts, will be dissipated. It is thus, and only thus, that Science can effectually banish Superstition.

## HOW TO INVESTIGATE.

To those who may be desirous to aid the investigation now in progress, a few suggestions of the best means of doing so will doubtless be welcome.

There is an erroneous impression that none but professional Psychics are to be found. In truth, Psychics are frequent in private life, and especially among children. There are few family circles in which they may not be discovered by patient experiment. As there is nothing in mind, person, or manner to indicate an organisation having such an excess of Psychic Force as to produce the phenomena of Psychism, its existence can only be discovered by trials repeatedly made with the same circle. The process is very simple. Not less than five nor more than nine should form a party, who should meet twice or thrice a week (the more frequently the better). Instead of lounging before the fire, they should seat themselves at a table, lay their hands upon it, and in that position continue their chat, mingled with music and song. It is as easy to'enjoy a social gathering seated thus as in any other grouping. If there is neither sound nor motion in the table in an hour, break up the circle, take tea, talk, and in half an hour re-form it—that is, if none are weary, for in such case the trial should end at once. There should be no disappointment if nothing comes, but it should be tried again and again, *always preserving the same circle.* If

one of the party is a Psychic, signs of it will probably
appear by the sixth sitting, and then it can be readily
ascertained who the Psychic is by each one in turn
quitting the circle, and thus discovering whose presence
is necessary to the action of the Force. As soon as
sounds and motions are presented, careful note should
be taken of the phenomena occurring at every future
meeting, and experiments and tests devised and tried
for the purpose of ascertaining the conditions under
which the phenomena appear, and thus to aid the
inquiry into their cause which is now being so ex-
tensively and actively pursued in all parts of the
country.

It has been calculated that about one person in thirty
is a Psychic in England, and about one person in
twenty in Scotland and America, the faculty being obviously much more powerfully developed in certain
races of men than in others. As I have stated above,
it is very frequent with children, and often disappears
from them entirely at puberty. Infants in arms are
sometimes Psychics, and there is said to be an instant
and marked increase of the Force when they are taken
into the circle or even brought into the room. In one
instance within my own observation the entry of a servant
with a message was instantly followed by a manifest
access of the Force, shown as the door opened, continu-
ing while she was in the room, and declining when she
left it. Where a child is a Psychic, it will be desirable
to ascertain the nature of the intelligence that then
directs the Force—if it is that of a child—and in the
case of an infant Psychic if any intelligence whatever is exhibited by the Force—and I shall be

greatly obliged by information of actual experiences on these points, whose importance will be obvious at a glance.

A table is not necessary to the operation of the Force. Any solid body that connects the persons forming the chain is equally efficient. But a table is found to be the most convenient subject for experiment, as it enables the party to be comfortably seated and to converse at ease.

## POSTSCRIPT.

Since these pages were printed, the *Quarterly Review* has made a second edition an occasion for publishing what is probably intended to be a confession of errors and an apology; or rather an excuse for its unjustifiable personal attacks upon the constructor and witnesses of a scientific experiment. It frankly admits the falsity of its assertion that Dr. Huggins and myself are converts to the creed of Spiritualism, but it has not the grace to express regret for the vilification in which it had indulged on that utterly false assumption.

The writer endeavours to excuse himself by stating that he was misled by an article in *The Spiritualist.* But how unjustifiable is the carelessness that could permit a man to write and print two pages of virulent personal abuse and insult of three gentlemen, based on no better authority than an anonymous paragraph in an obscure journal, when the writer had before him the original publication by Mr. CROOKES himself, a glance at which would have shown him not only that his assumption was false but that the fact was the very reverse.

But even this lame excuse cannot be accepted, for, in the abusive article, the reviewer actually cites a passage from the very letter in which I expressly and emphatically assert that the result of the investigation had been to satisfy me that there was *no* evidence to support the theory of Spiritualism; thus proving beyond question *that he had read my letter*, and therefore must have known, and did know, that I had repudiated the theory of Spiritualism when he deliberately dared to call me a convert to it.

But the carelessness—to use the mildest term—of the reviewer, is such that he cannot even correct one error without falling into other blunders. He states now that I reject both Spiritualism and the Psychic Force. The letter he cites is throughout a declaration of conviction that the Force exists as a fact, though its source is yet to be ascertained, and the proposal which gave it the name which has been universally accepted for it was mine!

I am, however, delighted to find, by a note appended to this "apology," "confession," "explanation," or whatever it may be termed, that the authorship of the article has been erroneously attributed to Dr. Carpenter. I had already ventured to express a doubt of its reported paternity, because I could not believe that a man of his scientific and professional status could so forget the gentleman as in a purely scientific controversy to be guilty of the mingled mendacity and meanness that pervade the personalities of the article in the *Quarterly Review*.

*12th December*, 1871.

STEREOTYPED BY LOVEJOY, SON & CO.,
15 VANDEWATER ST., NEW YORK.

www.ingramcontent.com/pod-product-compliance
Lightning Source LLC
Chambersburg PA
CBHW022141090426
42742CB00010B/1341